BUREAU SURELEVE

–FRENCH CONSTITUTION–
FRANCE

Dr Amrit Rattan K Baidwan- Macfarland

BSc Hons, LLB (J.D) DLP, LLM, PhD, NP (Scots Bar, UK).
School of Law- and Legal Practice -International law and Treaties.
ABERDEEN-EDINBURGH-SCOTLAND -UK

authorHOUSE

AuthorHouse™ UK
1663 Liberty Drive
Bloomington, IN 47403 USA
www.authorhouse.co.uk
Phone: UK TFN: 0800 0148641 (Toll Free inside the UK)
*   UK Local: (02) 0369 56322 (+44 20 3695 6322 from outside the UK)*

Published by AuthorHouse 10/14/2021

ISBN: 978-1-6655-9407-3 (sc)
ISBN: 978-1-6655-9406-6 (e)

Library of Congress Control Number: 2021921084

Print information available on the last page.

Any people depicted in stock imagery provided by Getty Images are models, and such images are being used for illustrative purposes only. Certain stock imagery © Getty Images.

This book is printed on acid-free paper.

This book is dedicated to

The President of India -Pranab Mukherjee – (1935-2020) Bharat Ratna – the Highest Civil Order of Excellence.

Emeritus Professor of Jurisprudence – David Carey-Miller, School of Law, University of Aberdeen, Scotland, U.K.

And…

Distinguished Professor C Pieters of the USA Constitution and Laws, University of Maryland -American Carey School of Law, Washington USA.

Distinguished Emeritus Professor, Gareth Powers, Constitutional laws, and Unconstitutional Takings Clause – Property laws, Carey School of Law, University of Maryland, USA.

French universalism and international law

En Ventre Sa Mere

So let us begin, what are French universal principles, and how are they evaluated under international laws, how do these impact constitutions and laws all over the world, and what is their significance as applied to the positive affirmative legislation, with reference to women getting elected to high office.

First and foremost, French universal principles evaluate international laws by taking two viewpoints, one of its national character and the other of international law dictates; how it aligns with the national characteristics and character of France. International law cannot be directly binding, although it may be influential and binding only if, it is validated by France's authorities, then only can international law be a superior force to national statutes. Procedures exist by which statutes can be reviewed, and then if befitting can be reconciled to international law; obedience to it, therefore is optional.

Article 54, states that if an international commitment contains a clause contrary to the constitution, then the council President or Prime minister and deputies can ratify or approve it by amendments to the national constitution – The council can refuse, if the constitutionality of the statutes in validate international law, on grounds of extreme contradiction, and if not, the constitutionality of statutes, review could on the converse invalidate statutes, to bring them in line with international law.

France allows abortion only under certain conditions, and the court can deny a statute that could be judged to be contrary to the right of life, protected by the second article of the European convention on Human rights, (Everyone is protected by law, and the right to life, cannot be intentionally denied). The council can analyse whether materially, there are inconsistencies between abortion under exceptional circumstances and the right to life. A court can refuse to consider the international text on the grounds, that violation of constitutional texts ensures it has no bearing, as legal validity under the French constitution. The council holds the condition of reciprocity effective, and its articles give validity to treaty terms within the French legal order, but the council can vary circumstances dependant on each case, dependant on the facts of each case.

The council reviews statutes a priori, before they are enforced and constitutional judges, judge their positions of knowing all the necessary facts (article 54, 1975).

Free access for all to elective positions gives the voters their justifications for effective choices. Differentialists fulfil these requirements by elevating equal and universal suffrage, and this enables paritary list of candidates, and in effect obliterates universalism and its values; equally it creates inbuilt prejudices against certain classes and is unable to grasp the common good. Affirmative concept does not exist for the benefit of women alone, it is argued, but for all citizens. Such texts occurrences have consequences. These changes are intensified by the fact that new provisions introduced in the legal order, are without limits in time. The change thus it is posited will be permanent not simply a correction of principle.

The constitutional council did not agree latterly with this argument and concluded that new constitutional provisions had modified old principles of universalism and that modifications were intended to permit the legislator to institute any mechanism to give effect to new laws, and as so far, as the legislative reconciles, the new constitutional rules and principles; from which the powers did not intend to derogate. It is too soon to appreciate the real consequences and effects of statutes under a changed constitution, departing from the principles of universalism.

These issues do not belong to France, alone in a universalistic system, sovereignty is national, belongs to the people, but French legal theory disagrees, and that representation dematerialises the questions of sovereignty, by displacing it onto a pseudo model of people's representatives. Elections then the purpose is to encourage the expression of national will consonant with common good, according to prevailing societal character and hence conceptions. This reasoning is justified and does not seek the legal exclusion of any persons from politics. The republic and democracy are distinct in that the latter qualifies each citizen to be entitled to an equal right of suffrage, their common goal is to demand,

Thus, ambiguities arise due to conflicts, created by the understanding of the law between universalists and differentialists. In France in 1994, 1999, 2000 acts were made to deal with equal access by women and men to elective offices and position and only minimal reform was required to the constitution.

Force Majeure

Constitutional validity

Statutes are referred to constitutional council and parliamentary opposition, which argues if a certain right was not required, by the constitutional amendment, which encourages equality, but does that then not as a rule, encourage differentialists distorting the true meaning, and substance of universalism. Mandatory paritary would distinguish negatively in those better qualified men would have to give up places to lesser qualified women.

In fact, cases, concerning gender have never reached the constitutional council. Political representation must be from all strata of society including minorities which includes women. Many rights are not mentioned in the declaration of rights and are purely legislative assertions. The right to birth control was authorised in 1968 and abortion in 1976; reinforced by statute. These laws have never been disallowed as unconstitutional. France responds to contradictions and difficulties of constitutional universalism, often. Constitutional amendment calls have been made to facilitate dynamic conception of equality and to secure rights of those society deems as a minority, i.e., women in France. There are contradictions and difficulties of constitutional universalism, by the application of modern feminist theory to law. Feminists launched movements to accommodate the constitutional council's interpretation of universalism and since others have used the ideal of paritary, entered debates to change positive law. This then became a model for the rest of the world.

The French constitution had altered constitutional control, by creating an organ to regulate the constitutionality of the laws, by limiting the power of legislature to disregard the constitution with certain limitations. The first limitation can arise from the procedures used to control constitutionality, and these intervene spaces prior to the adoption of statute. Once enacted, the text becomes law and has binding force and statutes, or codified law becomes indisputable. Courts defending cases, do not examine inconsistencies between codified laws, which rule each case and constitutional texts (rights declaration) which might contradict the statute and hence in France, it cannot be opposed and remains in force, unless laws are amended. The power to submit laws to the council are government members and citizens do not hold this power. Judicial review is a new introduction of control and the principle of universal application prevent differential application to different members of social strata. Laws make no distinction between men and women, or they would fall foul of the universal principle.

Argumentation adopted by constitutional councils are placed under scrutiny. There is a balancing act, between articles of the constitution fundamental rights and multilateral agreements, often it is difficult to obtain strict reciprocity and agreements are not always given full effect. Fundamental human right violations cannot be justified, through by stating these violations exist elsewhere. The EC on human rights is closely embedded in many institutions, including the European union, the courts, like conventions are considered to be part of European law and are also applicable to member states of the European union, the Luxembourg court. The constitutional council in the past has encouraged courts to enforce international law with the French legal system, when deciding ordinary cases, in point and principle, if there is inconsistency between international law and texts or acts relative for the case, and then consideration is given if a regulation of international law, has created rights, or whether the international law just provides directives for the state, letting legal authorities line up with the directives of the French courts. They differ in the way how international law applies to each case.

Certain states in the USA ban affirmative action, of selective employment. Texas had a ban on it, and there are twenty-nine states where affirmative action is legal. Affirmative action of America is a set of laws, policies, intended to end and correct the impact of discriminative practices, such that government mandated, approved, which exclude access to education and employment, mainly of racial minorities, and or women in certain type of high-profile jobs. The impetus is to redress disadvantages and to engage educational and government establishments and make sure they are representative of the populations they serve. Affirmative actions included quotas till the supreme court ruled them unconstitutional. The arguments in favour of affirmative action were to end discrimination, due to race, colour, creed, or national origins. Due to civil rights protections and affirmative action, percentage of women in professional zones increased, architects, doctors, lawyers, engineers, chemists, and university faculty professors, deans, and faculty heads in all departments. It was also done to counterbalance historic inequalities. However affirmative action has been subjected to scrutiny via court cases, and on constitutional grounds. Analysis was made using the elimination of bias, of artificially elevating students into schools, universities, they otherwise would not be capable of attending, resulting in high dropout rates, the idea of class inequality, was tested for minorities, African, Spanish, East Asian, Chinese, European Americans. Many lawyers, and supreme court justices, including Thomas, and others opposed affirmative action, and the thesis put forward was that the equal protection clause of the 14th Amendment, forbids consideration on purely race, which results in preferential treatment, and put forward the idea, that certain classes, groups, races, including the minority groups, or classes, require special treatment, in order to succeed; however in the United States, a prominent form of positive affirmative principle towards racial preference, has been instituted relating to access of education. Public polls vary on affirmative action, and some suggest that selection should be solely on merit, regardless of race or ethnicity. This argument is similar to that made by France on universalism embedded as constitutional principles.

Sharia in the Arabian Peninsula refers to immutable principles derived from higher laws (Divine natural justice precepts). It is contrasted with fiqh which refers to scholarly interpretations and there are in theory three of four sources, Quran (Sunna), Qiyas (analogical reasoning), Ijma (Juridical consensus) and authentic Hadith). All laws, rules, statutes, directives, are derived from immutable principles and must align with these and rulings are normally concerned with ethics, legal norms, and actions assigned to various categories, mandatory, recommended, neutral, abhorred, prohibited and some are as corresponding to living life, in accordance with God's will. The civil and commercial code overlap with the roman notions of law, and current western legal systems. Under New Saudi Arabia reforms women are now given more prominent positions and roles in administration and society.

The European Human rights are no longer merely a legal concept, they have entered the mainstream and have come to dominate the layperson's perceptions of legal rights and duties. The idea that certain rights inalienably attach to the status of humanity is not just a recent development, rights and duties define human society long before the formation of any state. The evil of autocracy was defined by the European wars under Hitler as the Arabian and Middle east wars were defined by the autocracy of Saddam Hussein. How do we define rights, how do we enforce them and against whom, how will we ensure they do not overwhelm each other? In Europe there have always been two schools of thought, the first from Hobbes, and the second through John Locke.

Locke was a utilitarian political scientist, and proposed that humans sought pleasure and avoided pain, and he argued that liberal empowering measures were sufficient to command good behaviour from humans, if they got what they wanted, they would be happy and hence no civil unrest would ensue.

Hobbs, however, orders that the state retain all rights, but those granted explicitly to citizens and residents.

The Lockean School proposes all rights are vested not by the state in citizens, and residents but by an overarching natural order and the state should therefore only retain the rights which it has specifically ruled to be retained by itself.

All charters granting rights therefore, dating from the Magna Carta to the present-day united nations declarations of human rights are Hobbesian charters. However, the American constitution is a Lockean charter. The human right Act 1998, incorporated the European convention on human rights into the domestic law of nations, including France and its domestic laws. It is part Hobbesian, part Lockean, and yet, there are a number of pros and cons, for example if the Hobbesian approach, is adopted, are liberal aspirations legitimate and if the Lockean approach is adopted, how can rights be appropriated by the state and could it then be curbed or arrested through major or extensive legislation.

After the second war, Europe was divided, and it laid bare the deep-seated hatred and animosity that ran through the politics and social life of Europe. The nuclear bomb dropped on Hiroshima and Nagasaki, gave this animosity an additional dimension of terror danger, threat to civic society. It is the same now after 20 years wars in the Arabian Peninsula and the middle east and this has created similar rifts in the societal structures. However, Soon the European council was established in Strasbourg France, in 1949. Harmonisation was essential to promote peace. It was founded to protect civil and political rights of the individual. The ECHR was divided into an overview and five sections. Article one, the enabling article, which commands obedience, by contracting states, section I, articles 2-18, list convention rights and their scope, section II-V consist of articles 19-59, these are procedural in scope and the protocols, involve amending sections, which have to be signed and ratified by contracting states as was the ECHR. Although no hierarchy was prescribed between convention rights, they are regarded as equally important by the ECHR. There are tests that must be passed before a right is breached and remedies are available.

Absolute rights cannot be derogated from, limited rights can under exceptions, and qualified rights derogation is permitted. Public emergencies that threaten life of the nation, and the measures must be consistent with obligations under international laws. Monist theory treats international law and domestic law as two parts of the same unit. Its dominant principle as doctrine of incorporation; the dualist theory treats international law and domestic as separate, its dominant principle is the doctrine of transformation. Much of Europe except France, shares a firmly entrenched monist tradition, and it is established public policy that courts give effect to clearly established rules of international law; however, they differ in how they give effect to customary international law and to treaty based international law.

Is the ECHR in domestic law constitutional law, the convention rights and responsibilities form a common set of binding values for public authorities right across France and public bodies must have human rights principles, when they make decisions, and must be part of policy making. In states that have no written constitution, the Human rights fills the gap and the absence of an all-encompassing written law to which all other laws, must be interpreted in order to conform, has marked key decisions.

The convention rights include freedom from all manner of discrimination in public, work and private lives, article 14, and this prohibits discrimination, it states the enjoyment of rights, and freedoms, set forth in the ECHR be secured without discrimination on any ground, sex, race, colour, language, religion, political or other opinion, natural or social origin, association with minorities, property, or status.

Article 14 prohibits within the ambit of the rights, and freedoms guaranteed discriminatory treatment as its basis or reason of person characteristic by which persons are distinguishable from each other. Public authorities state bodies are obliged to comply, and this applies to paritary rights, for women to be elected to high office towards equal representation, on legislative, executive and judiciary bodies of governance of statecraft.

Oyer et Terminer

European law includes convention on human rights – is differently adopted by French courts and although international law prevails over contradictory provisions, the final drawing conclusions arrive from the doctrinal paradigms of the French constitution. There can be no inconsistency under French law. The right to abortion is protected under the French laws and the European right to life there is no inconsistency as long as the right to abortion meets the requirements 10 weeks and consent but European law may be applied to the French but if it goes against French universalism, it will be challenged by France, prima facie if it creates formal irregularities it appeals to the ECHR values which rests on freedom and formal equality. The principle of equal treatment for men and women regarding employment training and promotion, meant France had to review its legal provisions protecting women and mothers.

What constitutes legal universalism, or republican universalism – it rests on a nation's constitution, and this reviews parliamentary acts for their conformity with the constitution including the principle of universality. This encourages clarity and uniformity in interpreting the constitution and discourages innovation. Contemporary positive law is rooted in French history, and the principle of universalism serves as a template for evaluating public policy including novel issues equating genders with equality. Constitutions established determine the way in which legal rights are then applied and resolved in legal systems. Human right revolutions often stem from discontent with society and with differing legal prerogatives and inequality that is formalised thus France did away with the notion of nobility, clergy and feudal states, and persons wanted social and legal recognition of wealth and prominence.

The old laws changed and responded to legal equality throughout France. This approach required emphasis on formalising equality before the law and not only on equality of condition. The laws were codified after the revolution.

Jury

The revolutions often raise the question of sovereignty, for enlightenment for contextual reasons, and to modify the theory of sovereignty. Revolutions amend the view of nation as the ultimate sovereign, and new conceptions are born of government and governed.

The jurisdiction of courts can be limited to enforce powers review the acts of other powers, these changing frameworks based on the principle of universalism has key components, the universal inalienable, natural rights of humans which implies the equality of all rights among persons without regard to considerations such as gender. The indivisibility of the republic, which significantly limits the possibility of legally recognising divisions among citizens. Whether natural or constructed, the principle of unity often reinforces the principle of universality of rights ensuring equality of all citizens before the law, categorizations are forbidden, and gives all citizens of all gender's equal rights. The formal equality of universalism does not exclude and may even require a legislative structure that respects all persons and protects their equal rights to participate in public life. The French rights man and of citizen, was a text designed to declare the aims of the revolution and define the natural unalienable and sacred rights of man.

Voir Dire

Legislation was secured to protect these rights, and libertarian values qualified those social destinations may be based only on considerations, of the common good albeit all are born, remain free and of equal rights. The law is often the expression of the general lock, all are equally eligible for high offices in public positions employment according to skill, education, ability and without other distinctions apart from their virtues and talents. Thus, a republic must provide for the guarantee of these rights, separation of powers, or the constitution fails.

A single article would not be sufficient to give the declaration binding force. If two revolutionary constitutions come one after another, the first will lose constitutional force, if the second is adopted and declares the first has no binding force. Both these reduce texts to a set of political principles without legal force. The declaration changes the adoption of a text if it comes directly at the end of a great event, like second world war. Often the preamble opens up with words that proclaim the intentions of the republic – later preambles maintain the constitutionality and proclaim it again and then confirm and complement the preamble and a chapter gives the council power to control the actions of the legislature benefiting the declaration.

Cy Pres Doctrine

The principle of universalism is the political inspiration and gained through full constitutional force for two centuries later. Constitution can be silent on specific questions and can be stated in general terms, that the law guarantees women equal rights with men in all spheres. The implementation of the principle of universalism changes the status of citizens and the legal status and is needs based.

The constitution's main focus is on regulating the relationship between federal and state governments, rather than setting out how citizens are to be governed at the micro levels. Judges find that the constitution was prepared in line with the concept of universalism, based on these principles as in France and that democracy was enshrined within these as laws and rights. The laws application followed, the Anglo-American systems, rather than the roman European one, and was set by the rules of common law developed in its jurisdiction. It was clear that drafting of the constitution, was driven by intent in the preamble same as in France and America and the legal order was hierarchical with the principles of the constitution leading as a fundamental thesis of universalism which dictated laws and allowed certain human rights whilst disallowing those forbidden by the norms of natural justice.

Part II

Indo-Orient - Pacific –
Australia and New Zealand

The Colonies of Australia and New Zealand first became commonwealth in 1901, and finally Australian women could vote in the elections. These formal developments gradually began to resemble those of France. In the light of current realities, the French system resulted in reforms in Australia. Then in 1999, France faced constitutional amendments. The obstacles could be avoided by adjustments to old models but as always, a constitution is very difficult to amend. There was political opposition to positive affirmative policies, these assisting mandatory quotas. Gender differences in high office remain over other forms of differences in a diverse nation. There were legal obstacles, the federal system is only one hundred years old, and it is unlike the French constitutional system, in that legislation can have its constitutional validity challenged in courts, and liberal rules exist to seek review.

The constitution's main focus is on regulating the relationship between federal and state governments, rather than setting out how citizens are to be governed at the micro levels. Judges find that the constitution was prepared in line with the concept of universalism, based on those principles as in France, and that democracy, was enshrined within these as laws and rights.

The laws application followed the Anglo-American systems rather than the roman European ones and was set by the rules of constitutional law developed in its jurisdiction. It was clear that drafting of the constitution was driven by intent in the preamble same as in France and America and the legal order was hierarchical with the principles of the constitution, leading as a fundamental thesis, of universalism, which dictated laws, and allowed certain human rights, whilst disallowing those forbidden by the norms by natural juristic thinking.

The concept of positive actions did not get within the Swiss legal order, and created anomalies, paradoxes which resulted in further inequalities, by merit of persons. Positive action or affirmative positive principle have a thesis to correct disadvantages of the past; requiring preferential measures when hiring people, however it also creates an exclusion principle. Should a state make distinction on merit or on gender, the question of tie breaks a case where two equally qualified candidates competing, preference is given to the woman by virtue of her gender. Swiss legal order does not recognise quotas and is monistic. The women's movement began in late seventy's and had snow balled, since then, the onus was to positively further the material equality between men and women in society. Swiss people rejected positive reaffirmation of women in high office.

The constitution, had to be amended to a strict 50% women in tack and that the conseil des etas would have a man and woman and in the conseil national as well, i.e. in both chambers of the federal assembly, equality was the rule of the day, they then waited, the conseil federal, the Swiss executive to be composed of 3 out of its 7 members and the tribunal federal, the Swiss supreme court of at least 40 women. The Federal council and assembly asked the people to reject the initiative and they offered no flexible options, the principle of equality lost. The council's view was that the underrepresentation of women in politics is a social problem and cannot be resolved by legal enforcement.

The council and parliament recommended that people reject initiatives, and quotas, their arguments were the following eliminating material distinctions – would create another formal one, quotas violate the right to be treated equally as other candidates with regard to gender. They infringe by Swiss constitution, liberty, and choice. Initiatives have a legitimate aim, they are restrictive under representation in politics is for social reasons, and in equalities are eliminated by legislators in political institutions. Women are not a minority and thus can further by other means their political representation, based on the principle of equality, the liberty to vote. Enabling devices are present in education and economic spheres. There is thus an absence of counter objections, positive measures cannot trample on other people's fundamental rights, and infringe their rights, and quotas do not promote equality, but are an illusion and create real discrimination.

Thus, the constitution was a higher norm, than laws and rights, and ensured the recognition, of fundamental principles, of human civil liberty rights, and precisely ordered, the capacity to enact non-discriminatory legislation aligned to these principles. Bad laws thus could be failed, challenged struck down or reviewed. There was a general commitment in the constitution, to substantive and formal equality which resulted through these same principles. However, this view was challenged, that there was no 14th amendment, as in the US constitution, or a developed notion of it. However, universalism is an aspect of French law which preceded both Armenian and Australian. The legislative path must be taken in constitutional development as stated by French judges, rather than a revolutionary one. The traditions in commonwealth systems, unlike Rome and France is a tradition, which accommodates deviation from certain ideals. Pragmatism rather than conformity to well established roman juristic ideals or those of Russia, China, India as ancient civilization, has been its watchword.

A system based on pragmatism thus faces few constitutional obstacles. Australian courts seldom consider constitutional validity of paritary systems. Factors like history, cultural norms, societal interests, minority representation are emphasized in legislative assemblies and there are examples of such consideration which justify departure from philosophical ideals and favour utility and pragmatism.

There are implied constitutional obstacles in the adoption of paritary and rights as in France and are inferred from the structure of constitution. The paritary system, leaves room, for all citizens to become candidates. Australia is party to the international covenant, on economic, social, and cultural rights, the convention on the elimination of all forms of racial discrimination against women, political rights of women under international law conventions, concerning discrimination in respect of employment and occupation. Under laws, the federal executive exerts its prerogative to enter treaties. The role is the essential in the treatment of obligations under international laws. Treaties do not become domestic law, unless incorporated by legislation, there are no distinctions, between treaties, executive agreements, and congressional executive agreement and executive power is limited to specific heads of power, those in relation to foreign affairs, the expression in international relations, has resulted in the Australian government to legislate treaties are based on constitutional fundamental principles, and legislation. Treaties envisage affirmative action, programmes and therefore legislation is enacted. The failures remain in prohibiting gender distinctions in applications for females to high office. Australian legal order, received, a little political support and voluntary measures were not implemented. The High court has indicated once objectives are achieved, legislation must cease. Most agree this is critical and what about the notion of overcoming built in prejudice that males are superior to females.

Europe - Spain, Bosnia

In Spain, the unmarried woman, has full legal capacity, but a married woman like the married man is a pillar of the family an indispensable person of moral reconstruction for the family and society. There is no higher status, as they serve as mother and teachers of their sons. The man is the breadwinner and the woman the defender of life in the home – in the end this defines them, and each a high and useful role. The ideology of Spain and Portugal is profoundly conservative, with a view towards family and society in which decisive decisions impact at political and legal levels. Thus, the constitution, stated all citizens were equal except women, due to differences in arising from her nature, women's political participation, persisted but the civil code 1967 changed everything with man as head of family, granting him the power to take decisions of home and family. Access to diplomacy and judiciary were strictly forbidden. Revolutions changed Portuguese and Spanish society. The principle of universality article 12 according to which all citizens shall enjoy the rights and be subject to the duties laid down in the constitution. The Principles of equality stated that all citizens shall have the same rank, are equal before the law (article 13 number 1) and no one shall be privileged nor favoured or discriminated against or deprived of any right or exempted from any duty of any right or exempted from any duty by reason of his or her ancestry, sex race, language territory of origin, religion political or ideological conviction, education economic situation or social circumstance (article 12 number 2). Thus, these principles are not competing and cancelling each other but are complementary, that all citizens have all rights and duties and on the other hand, that they all have the same, the importance of this analysis the inclusion of an express prohibition based on gender.

The legal domination explains this fundamental principle of equality, but there are many implications in the field of family, it states spouses have equal rights, to civil political educational capacities, and maintaining their family. These concerns extend to affirming principles of equal opportunity, with equal pay for equal work, with no inherent salary discrimination. The constitution recognises women are special and need protections during pregnancy and after childbirth. Effective equality needs positive measures to root out inequalities.

The fundamental text acknowledges that effective equality will need positive efforts to overcome equalities. The constitution grants rights to access for day nurseries, for children and right to family life and planning. This is a solid legal framework for equality under international law – and its articles amended those of the Rome treaty and European charter of fundamental rights. These traditional stereotypes are challenged, and individual mentalities moulded to the new norm. There is always the need to reconcile professional and family lives. Full equality would mean women could rule just as well as men, thus offering women the right to engage in political life and in foreign affairs.

However, there are objections to quotas and parity is seen as incompatible to the principle of republican universalism.

The universal and inalienable natural rights imply equality of right among all persons, and as such sovereignty granting all citizens, men, and women exactly the same rights to elect and be elected. If there is express constitutional prohibition of privilege, then the concept of parity is obliterated as unconstitutional. The court has repeatedly stated that the idea of equality cannot be interpreted in absolute terms and must be interpreted as a discretion, limiting discretion and no imposition of differentiation. Thus, formulation merges with promotion of equality and prohibition of discrimination. Election to the Portuguese parliament as such do not send contradictory messages, amendments introduced can amend electoral laws, and express greater actual equality, lay foundation for reforms and the political will is required to implement them.

Arabia and Middle East

Women in Israel in the Middle east, Arabian Peninsula have suffered extreme discrimination, and denial of their fundamental rights, it is deeply rooted in religious traditions. Women wished to embrace equality but in 1948, the declaration of independence was never given the force of law. Israel began its constitution late as1992 and made no specific mention to equality, but courts suggested it had been incorporated by implication. The Knesset enacted laws to realise equality, for equal salary, employment, diminished discrimination, but it failed to turn to affirmative action to remedy this imbalance. Finally, paritary rights entered politics and so despite banners women entered politics.

Belgians imitated the French, in life and politics, it adopted quotas for women, but laws were not passed as a matter of course, there were plans laid to amend the constitution to include equal treatment of men and women, and the political landscape began to change. International treaties, commonly ask contracting states to implement the principle of equal treatment of men and women. Principles on equality evoke as a result of ideology. In Netherlands, women cannot enter high political life, genuine equality is not realized. Through mandates, and legal scholars will remain busy for many more years to come.

Indo Orient Pacific - Asia Major, Orient – India – China

India was one of the first nations to have a female Prime Minister, Indira Gandhi, till today serves as an exemplar and a role model. Women in ancient India dating back in time Pre-history, were equal to their kings and rode alongside them in many a battle. Today India has continued this legacy in the corporate world, politics, aviation, and most of civic life. Women's contribution has been enormous, and they have never not been in the limelight of political life.

The Indian political system is a republic and a democracy – it is a continent with twenty-eight nation states and union territories under the control of a central federal government, elections are held every five years, and it has no law analogous to French law on mandatory parity. India's constitution guarantees both men and women equal rights in political participation. India has been culturally a traditional society, with a Patriarch as head of family, and yet women are celebrated those who show extraordinary resilience and courage. The legislative efforts attempt to secure greater engagement from women, there is no such thing as exclusively male constituencies. Representation of women and state level although law, women occupy some of the highest seats in government. Women's entry into politics is directly related to their emancipation. The women reservation Bill 1996 addresses women's role in the Lok Sabha and Vidhan Sabha.

Reservations are allocated to scheduled castes and scheduled tribes and these manner of reservation aims to better representation of women from all stratas of life. These initiate anyone that bills grant special privileges to elect women, and on the grounds of social justice all women are not taken on board. These arguments reflect current realities, and it has substance due to past experience, women in public life indicating that India does not hold women back in leadership roles if they possess these attributes. Indian society favour women political participation and women often develop a political base. Politics in India is a clean profession and well respected and political deliberations continue to draw women of excellence to political life.

In China like France, paritary rights alone will not give women a real opportunity to run for office. Equality is continually enriched by the development of society. Social equality emphasizes the social dignity of all citizens forbidding discrimination or prejudice. Reviving the history of human society, we can see that all the citizens in the republic of China are equal before the law after the foundation of the people's republic of China, article 33 and 34 all citizens will have the right to vote and be elected to public positions. Women's interest in Politics has steadily increased, particularly at the highest levels.

In China as in other nations of the world, gender discrimination still takes place, economic development has changed society, and there is less breach of the equality principle. The long march from formal equality to substantive equality will take years of cultural change and careful legislation and so inequality will be reduced. Yet Aung San Suu Kyi was elected her head of state in Myanmar and latterly as its foreign Minister, of oriental background.

Sweden Tunisia Senegal Ukraine -Western and Eastern Europe, Africa.

Thus, French politics has been embraced in Sweden, in Tunisia and Senegal. Several lines of thought can be distinguished the enlightenment view, as expressed by the principle of universalism, which prevent constitutional references to gender origins and petty differences. On the other hand, the plurality of interests, results in changing the paradigm and affirmative action's results in differing positions.

Ukraine women in particular did not develop to the same extent as their western counterparts, but this was prevalent throughout Ukrainian society and much of the eastern bloc nations. Persons of both genders, male and female under the roman and Germanic legal systems, were considered legally competent and were capable of progressing without a trustee. During the post war era women's legal status was supported by statutes and equality was introduced into both criminal and civil articles. Both genders were subjects to the same laws and regulations and no restrictions were imposed on one gender and not the other. The constitution, of eastern bloc countries suffered grave historic injustices, some lost their independence and got absorbed by other states and legal status became differential and difficult. Austria took over Ukraine as its neighbour nation and civil law proclaimed the mentally incompetent blind, deaf at pace with women, unable to testify to their own wills on death.

France her universalism, constitution and rights allowed and disallowed by her laws, the framework for many European nations who imitate this formulation and endorse the right of both person men and women if they are able to participate in the formulation of government policy and the right to hold public office and represent their country at an international level. Ukraine has made an effort in recent times to promote persons of both genders, including women to participate in government through elected office, via act seven-eighths of their convention against discrimination able persons with merit of either gender from holding elected office. France serves as a model for an egalitarian society, with established republican traditions, rule of development, and well-developed corpus juris, body of laws, regarding positions on highest offices of the land. Women's role from housekeeper to office worker has gradually changed over the last few decades. Ukraine gains its traditions and history from Russia and has a history of education, women that goes back as Russian was then Soviet Union, and unwritten rules concerning women visited with in legislative bodies. The principle of universality was formulated mandatory like France all were equal, before the law which was over and above the equality of condition proposed in the 2020's. The first past the post principle applied status of genders, reflects the circumstances of a country under political change from totalitarian to liberal republic or democracy. Ukraine as a transitional state has present many contractions, in the sphere of elected offices for both persons but there is a clear tendency towards adopting universalism in its constitution and other laws. Women are protected from dangerous jobs such as iron processing fineries, but Ukraine is far behind in the system of proportional representation, of the best of males and the best of females in the top positions.

The passing of laws for elective office based on equality in France – is a victory for activating this principle in other parts of the European sphere. France places emphasis on universalism over differentialism, the constitution, which constitutes key amendments articles and principles which for the basis of rights allowed and disallowed and the passing of laws, instruments, and codified statutes out with these republican concepts, democracy nor human rights can prevail as standalone structures. Prevailing values differed from culture to culture, tradition to tradition, throughout the world, that men are perceived as precise, decisive, steady calm, disciplined organised, scientific logical, reasoning, adept at argumentation, good at risk analysis, independent ambitious, inclined to a natural sense of leadership, self-satisfied, confident, clear headed, combative, objective good at theoretical ideas and concepts flair for politics, law, administration, governance, sceptical sensible, is true of many men, but not all, the traits of women as talkative, affected, vain, shallow, gossipy, frivolous, sly, indiscreet, subservient, unstable scheming, are true of some women not all, either or are traits which belong to men and women or persons who have evolved through education, application, experience.

The concept of universality relates to these and deals with both in unique ways, women with calibre and potential as men stood high on electoral lists not because of their class in gender but that they have the merits to be involved at the top of the political circles.

There are several arguments for classic universalism, and these are put forward so results land in the right box and not in the wrong box.

The introduction of positive affirmation realised the principal equality without negating quality and merits of person, it creates the environment necessary for the realisation of both on an equal footing from society comprising now both talented educated men and women with potential. In the modern in environment in Bosnia men hold power and retain it legally without considering women but breakthroughs into the political system can only be addressed through parity, to raise the political profile of women. Political parties in the mail should have sufficient number of women as well as men. This ensures a critical mass of women to influence decision making process; experience and leadership of both persons is necessary in political life, a genius can sit and abide in any bottle – political parties determine who is elected, so it is important for women to become electoral candidates in the first place.

No exception should be made for women if they lack the pre-requisites and the principles of universality must reign over equality, so it effects no violence is done to persons of ability – the idea of paritary, would be unacceptable, if the quality of persons in both is not respected, and inclusion should not be merely for a person's sex. This enables the implementation of better and more able candidates. Provisions such as these undermine the overall structures of universalism principles and rights.

There is however a broader context for a consideration for a greater practical equality. It can be viewed in the broader context by notions of universalism. Women's absence from political life and bodies is problematic.

Some legal norms are universal, but implies women are not in politics on the basis of universalism but are involved in politics on the existing male model and must fit into the existing male forms.

Bosnia is a country in transition, and has a history of Russian rule, which included the official ideological and legislative equality of both genders. Mass free education, significantly altered lives in former Yugoslavia, Bosnia, and the construct of equality, led to altered ideological economic and political circumstances, the terminology adapted to include men and women, but there remained a discord between constitutional and true reality

However, in recent elections, 26 % women were in the house of representatives, and local levels 20 % their arguments against quotas were the forcible positions of women in politics, should be only imposed as men through their knowledge, and abilities, under existing canons of constitutional and legislative equality, and so quotas were a form of legalised discrimination. The political culture has shifted from a predominantly male culture, and in the 2000's changed to election rules meant that women were not to be handicapped.

Results compared with earlier times, and political parties now manifest high calibre women greater than 50%. The French example has stimulated change in other European countries as well.

In Switzerland, France,it is prevalent, and the principle of regime of equality exists;It has been guaranteed by article 8 of the constitution, 1999, and most cantonal constitution's guarantee equality. The legal order is monistic and international law is binding for the nation.

The mandate article 8 mandate requires that the legislator eliminate all discrimination on ground of sex from existing legislation and adopt al necessary measures to further legal and material equality between genders.

Thus France, could create a new form of universalism to allow certain distinctions, which could be justified on the grounds of necessity and still promote equal opportunity for men and women.

The 2020's require equal access by women and men to elected offices and positions. France must contain equal numbers of men and women – to be elected for office. Thus, an innovative mode created to secure political equality for women in Europe, bolstered by proportional representation. This violates the French traditions, of republican universalism and the declaration of the rights of man and of citizen, which asserts equal rights of all human beings, before the law regardless of gender. Positive affirmation has been disallowed by France as this is deemed contrary to universalism principles. France its history begins with universal principles, and all rights wheresoever they stem from must first be reconciled with universal rights and then with treaties international rights and domestic human rights.

Benazir Bhutto – Pakistan Asia Major

Benazir Bhutto returned to her nation, 18th October 2001, she was a character and there were there were many contrasts between her and her father, Zulfikar Ali Bhutto, prima facie there appeared no weakness in her political strengths. She was dominant during the affliction in Afghanistan, Iraq war, and troubles in and around Pakistan. During her father's reign there were moments that defined a generation constant military Marches and he ruled with military and democratic might. The nations lay geographically between two wars middle east and Afghanistan. She renewed alliances to meet the threats of the 21st century and tried to democratize Pakistan. She stood at a moment of great challenges. Musharraf was canvassing and Pakistan an Arab Asian nation due to the war in Afghanistan on terrorism had to stand along her world allies, European American, Russian, Chinese, Japanese, Asian and Australia. The world had to rally together against new global threats, on climate change, oil dependence, extreme poverty, disease, pandemic genocides, and the world, failing states, death, and destruction. Under these fundamental challenges and Pakistan's beleaguered history, saving jobs, helping communities through tough times, was a daunting task. Exorbitant interest rates were making landowners unstable; and amid American and

European confusion, regulating borders. Foreign markets, trade and globalisation, tax breaks for companies, were all on her plate. The greatest threat to her nations security, securing intelligence services, network intelligence services, networks across the globe, from the act of dangerous weapons, cyber alliances, n Pakistan's infrastructure were all models that resulted from chaos and anarchy, and global conflicts. The fight against AL Qaeda, was at her doorstep, and the focus of the world was on Afghanistan. Bush and Cheney with NATO had engaged in war with no endings.

After 8 years in exile in Dubai and London, she returned to her people's political party. She declared her candidacy, in Larkana constituency, in November 2007, the state of emergency had been lifted her opposition Nawaz Sharif. She began travelling the country offering her manifesto in grand speeches, the campaign about reclaiming meaning of common purpose. Her primary return to Jinnah international Airport. She was homeward bound to heal the rifts. But suddenly there was a loud bang outside her vehicle, it was a terrorist suicide bomb attack. She was moved quickly to safety. Fifty people were dead, but she was not deterred from her campaign trail. She was an alumni of Radcliffe college at Harvard university and an oxford graduate, in Politics. A profile anti-abortion campaigner she led many meetings at the council of women world leaders. Her father Zulfikar too was President of Pakistan a reality she had lived.

On 27th December 2007, on her campaign trail, she swept past waving crowds but at Liaquat National Bagh, she was attacked again, and she was hit she collapsed, and died, instead of a victory at Rawalpindi, her nation mourned her sudden death. Benazir Bhutto became a victim of the war on terrorism and the winds stirring, were abrupt and her second return ended in violence and death.

Indira Gandhi - India Asia Major

She triumphed in the unification of India, reasserting its dignity and character pre-history and began a dynamic diplomacy, and resumption of defensive measures making India safe from capture from any external forces. She studied Khrushchev's doctrines for peace and noted the failures of the USA in collapsed summit conferences post world wars, she noted the breaks between major nations in the pacific Moscow and Beijing (Beijing), and USA's abortive interventions in the Congo.

She helped reshape the United Nations, through the advent of many administrations in the Indo-pacific – Atlantic worlds, and the attempts by nations, to prize away other nations contained after the world wars.

She took her advocacy to Cuba, to Arabia, some successes some ending chapters of the history of humankind, the continuing embroilment of the Atlantic nations in Asia which she brought to international desks.

She engaged in the real issues of pacts, blockades, the European defections, deadlocks, and arms race, she advocated for movement to unification using the classic models of ancient

India and restoration of sovereignty of European nations, including Germany.

She used her administration to adjust to new responsibilities, the situation stemming down from the 1950's and problematic military policies, and the growing threat from the Atlantic overextending containment only towards Asia and Indo China, France being replaced by the USA.

She grappled with the repercussions for Russia after the death of Stalin his succession and the attitude of the Russians and Russian relations with India. She attempted to reverse draconian policies which had led to multitude crisis post the world wars and 1947 – 1956.

She created the four-way method which she expounded at the Geneva Conferences, visits of Khrushchev and Bulganin and the crisis beginning in the Suez, by ambition and dreams of utopia. She knew it was trying to assign a single cause to any long history of a nation's expansion or withering and no society must bear constant mortal fear, she produced a simple open innocent and guileless society and it polarised the world into two parts, She understood the restoration of the balance of power, doe s not lie in any single domain and can neither be conscious nor a proclaimed objective. Indo -Pacific in the main China Myanmar generated the post war balance.

France had restored many families of nations and she understood its role as well as India's as indispensable to the balance.

Germany as a successor regime was not restored immediately but she knew a stable international system could not be established without Germany nor enduring peace would ensue.

The consequences of the world wars saw the rise of a new India both profoundly antagonistic to the status quo represented by Atlantic and some payee nations, peace truce to survive must be by virtue of a stable equilibrium not unstable equilibrium of weakness.

By contrast Atlantic became a closed society, a secret society, under the ideation of exceptionalism but Indo pacific was driven, suddenly, India finds herself defenceless on all sides. They were without frontiers exposed to attacks by titular peoples in the northeast, northwest and south.

And then again suddenly on a darkling plain, Ashoka descendants were swept with confused alarms of struggle and flight of theft grand theft where ignorant men entered to clash by nightfall.

Indira knew the history of India, for ten centuries and ten millennia, and that Indians, now find themselves in their first great continent, uninhabited through its vast and natural wilderness. How could this be.

For two centuries, Indians were surprised, survived but the phoenix had to be reborn again moving away from Kashmir to the central plains of New Delhi. The hammer blows finally ceased after the world wars and India with her land, people gathered up after a terrible sacrifice, the innate strength of the Indian lands and people.

In the first centuries of the Brahma era, beginning in the Himalayas, a sort of explosion occurred in enlightenment terms, among Kings and peoples inhabiting the Kashmir regions and caused an outpouring of thought in all directions at once, North, west, east, and south, and as far in the far east as Japan. The peaceful emperors of Mahabharata lay dumbstruck at the pouring of light from crystal fountains, it swept over them burning, them purifying them, every soul was touched, purified, and cleansed. Indira's soul was craved in this most potent and soulful place in India. After Millennia of peaceful reign, development of national and international instruments of governance and wisdom, were forged, India's fame spread throughout the world and invaders began to enter India.

The emperors disappeared in due course only to be replaced generation after generation by a fresh wave of invaders, the golden horde, seeking India's wealth to possess it as their own. The original Brahmins and their emperors and Kings of states were victims of successive invasions. The original Hindus lay defenceless on the plains near the Brahmaputra Ganges and Indus rivers.

History repeated itself again and again bursting out from the same sources scorching the earth, and when the assaults were over, the land littered with the dead bodies of many million, then the brutal tide lost steam, and finally began receding, facing great opposition, violent even, on all sides. So, in the face of continual assault and defeat, assault and defeat, India would emerge to fulfil Kashyap's prophecy, a giant nation under the sway of one woman, Indira, holding in her hands the destinies of the Indo Pacific and the Indo Atlantic, nearly half the world.

Eisenhower was a close friend and ally of India, and his ventures in the late fifty's promised to put pressures on nations destabilising India, and those failing to ratify treaties to that effect.

She was a person of determined purpose who let nothing stand in the way of her goal realisations. India was then a translational nation, and she had to concentrate on it exclusively and for larger considerations.

There was no neutrality on difference, native to Eisenhower's and successive Presidents, minds but to strengthen and reaffirm India and her state procedures were such whereby an organised team of subordinates prepared decisions that her commanding officers adopted as their own for the defence of the Indian borders and wider regions.

The communications post world wars had a decisive impact on the kids, pacific – although there were momentary set ups, but unanimous decisions were made by cabinet and in the Atlantic the European nations fell out, Russia, Spain were not invited, and Moscow's interdiction of acceptance aroused resentment among nations working on formulations. Moscow rejected proposals would not be moved, by the demonstrations, of servitude.

India forbids acceptance, mutual opposition doctrines were established, and various formal declarations of war followed in the Indo pacific.

IN the combat, there were truces, there were parleys diplomatic manoeuvres, of various sorts, there were intervals of relative relaxation to recover, and only temporary accords of a tactical nature were made – there was no real peace, for a while, but India was symbolised as content in her own continent and domain post war conferences and focused on her own recovery.

The conflicts in the Indo pacific never became history, Hiroshima and Nagasaki was a crime against humanity, and the French rejection of the EDC created a crisis throughout the pacific world, as its unification was left in disarray, the US-French alliance became a kind of possessors of Japan to assuage their guilt and that had not suffered perpetual condemnation unlike other nations post world wars.

Unification with its promise was wrecked by a combination of capitalism and communism equal measure. The disappointment and bitterness of the Indo pacific was palpable. Months of agitated diplomatic consultations ensued culminated in a conference of the Indo pacific powers, India, China, Japan and Russia and their saving commitment mitigated the crisis. China, Japan, Korea Russia continued to maintain mainlands of Indo Pacific the effective strength of force multipliers supreme allied commanders' division tactical air force, many treaties that despite neglect did not crumble completely. Gandhi connected with the universalizing, themes of pacific idealism she gained from ancient doctrines and those that proclaimed objectives of the liberty of lands and seas, making the world Ashoka's egalitarian model, not equal but egalitarian, and thus manifested only in the pacific world wars. With these concepts Peace was an ideal realised and the pacific bound together in a common egalitarian way unaware of the things to follow, breaches of their common hemisphere. She inherited a lot from her father who was her mentor and his legacy she inherited as her own brief. The Nehru-Indira foreign policy became the dominant foreign policy of the new shifting governance of India, like France before her from Monarchical, (whilst retaining certain features like the House of Lords (Rajya Sabha) and the House of commons (Lok Sabha) – into a Republic. The President then retained the Symbols and emblems of Emperor Ashoka in his office at Rashtrapati Bhavan Palace, in New Delhi. India then governed through her republican constitution, much like France did with a new order established after the end of Monarchical rules of governance. Indira like her father before her felt a nation's policy is shaped by its position in the world, its geographical position, the Indo Pacific sphere, in Asia-Orient Major, her history, and all these aggregates, then created a novel paradigm of foreign policy. India's prominent role therefore was in the Non-aligned base, building up developing countries post world wars, and also through the Indo pacific cold wars, involving major nations. She engaged with Cuba, Middle east, Afghanistan, Cambodia, and African nations. She continued to establish bilateral indo-us educational foundations, but under Nixon, the Indo-US relations became strained, and the Pokran Nuclear test made matters worse. This established India overnight as a nuclear-powered nation, and she entered and engaged with international nuclear treaties. Summits with Nixon, Reagan, USSR continued unabated, and with Nepal, Bhutan and newly formed Bangla Desh. She quickly introduced the Indira Doctrine, to consolidate all Himalayan nation states of India, as well as Nepal and Bhutan who aligned with India. Sikkim nation state was reincorporated back into India, after a swift referendum. Gandhi continued to support Palestinians in the Arab-Israel conflict, and India-Persia (Iran) renewed their Partnership under the Shah. She endorsed the ZOPEAN declaration, in Asia Pacific and was decorated by an Honorary Doctorate by Fiji nations.

Her Indo African foreign policy blossomed, and she re-established a bilateral geostrategic presence, there and became a vocal political voice against Apartheid in South Africa. She continued to establish great partnerships in Germany, Austria, UK with Willy Brandt, Edward Heath and Margaret Thatcher. She was assassinated and died young but left behind her legacy as modern-day foreign policy, based on the original Ashoka's Arthashastra principles – she followed these tools, of diplomacy, as a means for furthering peace, stability, and good international relations, as well as to mend disagreements, through resolution documents and formulation of treaties and international instruments and agreements.

Asma Al Assad – First Lady of Syria Arabia – Middle East

Asma Al Assad was born 11 August 1975 in London, to Fawatz Akhras, a cardiologist and her mother was a diplomat. She graduated from King's college London with a first-class honours Batchelor of Science degree in computer science and a diploma in French literature. Asma moved to Syria in November 2000 and married Bashar in December of that year. She became a policy advocate and head of the Syrian Trust development, which was connected to several charities for good works in Syria.

She took progressive position on women's rights and education. She came to prominence in 2011 when the Syria civil wars began in full earnest, before then very little was known about her or even about Syria. However, what was the political background through which she became known and what changes were happening in Syria and much of the Arabian Peninsula and the Middle east.

Since 2014, the change in the international paradigms in the Middle east arrived in the form of civil unrest and then Russia. The Syria civil war had become a multisided conflict in Syria between Russia, Iran and Ba'athist Syrian party, the Arab Republic, led by President Bashar Al Assad and other domestic allies and various domestic foreign forces i.e. USA, UK, EU, Australia, Canada and New Zealand, opposing both the Syrian government and each other to different degrees and in various spheres, via different strategies, tactics and combinations that are innovative, novel and never used in traditional warfare.

The initial paradigm did not involve Russia but was unilaterally, dictated by US and allies in the region, including Syrian opposition parties. Thus, the classic balance of power doctrine was not operating and became functional only through the entry of Russia, into the fray of the civil war, of Syria in the Middle East.

The civil war in Syria is part of the wider wave of the Arab unrest, conflicts, spilling over from the wars, in Libya, Iraq, Gaza Palestine, Afghanistan, Yemen and other parts of Africa, northern eastern and central. The Arab spring all over the African-Arab continent and spilled over and culminated in the Arab spring in Syria in the year 2011.

The Arab spring movement, constituted members, from all over Arabia, especially, the conflict zones and equally spilling in from Egypt, Libya, eastern, western, and central Africa, as well as other conflicts, in the middle east from 2011- 2019, i.e., Iraq and Yemen.

The Syria Arab spring claimed they were discontented with the Syrian government, and their collection of groups, demanded regime change and called for the removal of Assad as President.

Thus, amidst the chaos of the Middle east conflicts, a new wave of unrest began, and the Assad Government, moved quickly to contain the unrest, such that Syria's government and the state of Syria, would not collapse and fall.

The two sides engaged in Syria's conflict Russia and her allies and USA, and her allies held different perspectives about the Syrian civil war, since 2014 as he evolving situation warranted, and each side, developed different viewpoints, stances, paradigms, justifications, to support their political opinions.

The civil war was particularly suppressed, until the unrest marched into the capital of Syria, which is Damascus and Aleppo, and various violent tribes, factions, and groups, melted into the Arab spring and began to fight within these regions against Assad and against each other.

The Syrian army began to flounder, in the face of such organised and well developed assault by armed factions, the Sunni opposition rebel groups, the freedom Syrian army, Salafi Jihadist groups, the Nusra front, the mixed Kurdish Arabs, Saudi Arab groups, Sunni Militia groups, Syrian democratic forces and the Islamic state of Iraq and Islamic state of the Levant, with various prominent countries, in the region supporting the factions and armed groups, either directly or indirectly with, arms, ammunitions, money and supplies.

Several armies entered the fray with the US and allies who held a seminal argument about regime change, latterly Russia, activated the cold war balance of power doctrine and instituted a novel paradigm of containment by conversion of radical groups of civil unrest in Syria and reasserting its doctrine of right to protect.

Russia formed forces with Assad's government and thus prevented the fall of Damascus and Aleppo primarily and it proclaimed this via its diplomatic venues MFA Russia on public channels such as e-diplomacy twitter, as well as by its officially released documents in December 2017.

So how did this all come about, what were the key events that wrung in changes to the entrenched Middle East paradigms since 2001.

Russia loosely connected with BRICS, (Brazil, India, China, and South Africa), after it was ousted from the G8 nations, of which it was once part, and which was officially reduced to G7 nations and strongly connected with Syria, Iran, Hezbollah in Lebanon. It then entered the fray to support, the Syrian Arab republic government and Assad and the Syria armed forces militarily, as they were about to collapse in Damascus and Aleppo, due to the growing strength of the anti-regime forces.

Russia began to conduct airstrikes and other strategic military operations in September 2015 and the US led international coalition in Syria since 2015, shifted its stance from the removal of Assad and his regime.

Under Obama and Kerry administrations, a shift in foreign policy, was declared and refocused, on countering ISIL and an open declaration of this policy was made once Russia began supporting the Syrian government.

US Led forces conducted airstrikes against ISIL with Arab nations, and with western allies, but equally government and pro-government areas were accidentally hit. Special forces artillery units were sent into Syria to counter ISIL, by Anglo American governments.

The USA perspective and dynamic, was from the start dramatically opposed to Russia and both sides openly, vociferously supported their agenda with the US Supporting the democratic federation of Northern Syria and its armed wing SDF, and the Syrian militia armed forces, through military support, finances, and personnel and with trainers in logistics.

Russia held a diametrically opposed view to the US and endorsed Syria under the right to protect doctrine and principle. Turkey equally engaged actively, with the Syrian opposition, which with its support, began to occupy large swathes of north-western Syria, whilst still engaging significant ground fought battles against ISIL, SDF (Syrian Democratic forces) and its newly formed DPNS or structures.

Through all these changes in the political hemisphere, a serious blow was dealt to her person, during the intensity of the civil war, and in 2012 the European union froze her assets and placed a travel ban on her and other close family members, the same was repeated in 2020, latterly. In March 2021, the UK police headquarters, opened an international enquiry or investigation against her husband President Assad, and more sanctions were applied on Syria.

Through all this her health suffered immensely, and she developed breast cancer, but later was declared cancer free. She is likely to continue to play a key role in the Syrian political arena, despite setbacks. She has three children from President Assad, who too have lived through the civil wars, and it is now with her health returned, she is likely to continue to play a key role in the Syrian political arena.

Aung San Suu Kyi – Mayanmar – Burma

Aung San Suu Kyi was propelled into the history of Myanmar, by being the child of a President and distinguished political parents. After the assassination of her father, she decided to try and run for presidency of Myanmar. Overnight she was transformed from being the daughter of the famous General Aung Sand, into the first female President Elect. The public attention drawn to her plight under the Military Junta, who put her under house arrest, on trumped up charges, has exceeded those of any President in living history save Mahatma Gandhi and Nelson Mandela.

Yet as her disastrous rise to presidency neared expiration by the Military Junta, Aung San Suu Kyi, in a nation itself under siege, came into pre-eminence unique in her time, and emerged in a cacophony with people of the ilk and stature of Abraham Lincoln, Mahatma Gandhi and Martin Luther King all rolled into one. A few hours after the voting, and the thump of a resounding democratic victory, came her oppressive arrest. It had been Aung San Suu Kyi's darkest moment, while the world yet again floundered as planes for her imprisonment process hurtled down the tracks, braking in deafening screeches and came only to a halt when she was put under house arrest for fourteen years.

Many international leaders had met with her shortly after the death of her husband Michael Aris an Oxford Don, who had urged her to enter politics in Myanmar. It is believed after intense examination political and emotional, she had at first rejected the idea. It is also believed that she had been equally close to her father the President and her mother the first lady of Myanmar and had found it hard to adjust to the hatred and enmity engendered by her principles, morality, and participation by the extreme Military Junta.

Michael Aris a forthright and sensitive Englishman who died at the age of fifty-three of prostate cancer, had presented her with all the obstacles of the course, and she had entered the fray by being a willing and motivated candidate, just as her father had been before her. She had as a young political candidate demonstrated extraordinary capability for change and personal growth.

It is believed she had never really aspired to office, despite all the chatter of the world press and entreaties of close friends and family who wanted her to run. She had looked forward to a peaceful life with her husband Michael and her two sons, to a life with books, policy advocacy and becoming the head of a foundation or so in Myanmar.

Michael and her marriage proved to be an uninterrupted dialogue of ideas and aspirations and a lasting love – often punctuated by long absences due to the intervention and interference of the Burmese ruling government.

The Journey of Aung San Suu Kyi has been a trek across a political landscape in which she has always intended to inspire the expansion of her country's social consciousness, based on her own moral ideas and ideals and those of her generation, her Buddhist upbringing, with her inspiration being India's Mahatma Gandhi and his policy of pacifism. There is no question from the literature surrounding her relationship to Michael Aris that each had come to regard the other as the brightest star in the universe, the fusion of energy and purpose was never about him and his work as a Don at oxford but about them and the art of the possible.

Aung San Suu Kyi, lived up to the faith Michael had in her and has single handed changed Burmese awareness and will not doubt in its history. Though her opponents and enemies have grown more hostile and outraged as she has quietly in her own way marched up towards an insurmountable summit; unbowed by the humiliation of the military junta and unfazed by dangers, perils, military arrests and ambushes, attacks on her person and personality, that would have felled lesser mortals. Her journey is Odyssean and one the world has never witnessed and never will again.

When in time, the definitive history of her journey is written, it will be the most essential and yet elusive and dynamic of a Burmese presidency that shifted the sands of time, gearing often into bad times, occasionally into the good; but never for long. It will be difficult for the world to address and handle such an amazing phenomenon as Aung San Suu Kyi factor. For the first time in world history and politics, has a female president elect exposed political oppression and sent it off the rails.

Her Buddhist faith, of always doing all the good, one can, by all the means you can, in all the places you can, at all the times you can, if you ever can, had no doubt carried her through. Her life has been hard and arduous with many disasters which have arrived unexpectedly at her door.

Aung San Suu Kyi has always believed that her peaceful protestations about the most devastating acts of the Military Junta, would cause the ground to crumble beneath them. At the lowest point in her life with the loss of her husband, friend, and mentor; she returned with a vengeance to redeem her country's lost legacy.

She has thrown her weight and intellect into the battle to survive her ongoing crusade. In her passions, her fury and anguish she has convinced the world of what can be achieved by singularity of focus and purpose. Her credentials are of a person who is extraordinary, a colossus and a political stalwart, uniquely positioned at this moment and time in Burma's history to salvage true democracy, fundamental freedoms, and human rights.

Seen in the light of Burma's turbulent history since independence in 1947, Aung San Suu Kyi's ascent seems more remarkable and her endurance needs no description, or her iron will and disposition in the face of overwhelming odds against her.

Aung San Suu Kyi moved on after getting her Nobel Peace prize in 1996, through many attacks, house arrest, long periods under detention, wading her way through anti-government protests, various trespass incidents, to then become the State Counsellor and foreign Minister finally from 2016-2021.

Accusations were levied against her for violence against Rohingya Muslims and refugees and in 2021 she was arrested again, and placed under a new trial, deposed by the Myanmar Military along with other leaders of the National league, and the general election results were declared fraudulent.

ON April first, 2021, and latterly 12 April 2021, she was charged with an offence, violating the official secrets act, and another under section 25 of the natural disaster management law. On 10th June 2021, Suu Kyi was charged with corruption a much more serious change bought against her, which carries a heavier sentence, and the trial commenced on 14th June 2021, and if found guilty, she would be barred from running for office ever again.

Angela Merkel -Germany Europe

Angela Merkel the German Chancellor through the conflicts was noted as the most prominent politician on the global stage. She was born in Hamburg Germany in 1954. Merkel was the chancellor of the federation of Germany and was declared the leader of the free world, her foreign policy during the conflicts were to strengthen European co-operation and international trade agreements. She has also been declared widely de facto leader of the European union, throughout her tenure as chancellor. She presented her portfolio at fourteen G20 summits and hosted the twelfth G20 Hamburg summit. She enjoyed good relations with George W Bush and Barack Obama Trump and stated that Germany and America are tied by values of democracy, freedom and respect for the law and human dignity, independent of origins or political and religious views. She later changed her statement in 2017 declaring US was no longer held as a reliable partner of the EU. She has a good relationship with Russia and expressed concerns about over reliance on Russian energy and criticized new US sanctions against Russia, and EU Russia energy projects including the Nord Stream 2 gas pipeline. She supported the association between Ukraine and the European union. In October 2020, Merkel who had invited as the first European leader war refugees into Germany, urged them to integrate into German society and was in favour of mandatory solidarity mechanism for relocation of asylum seekers from Italy and Greece to other member states as part of a long-term solution to refugee influx from conflict zones.

Swaraj – India Asia Major

Sushma Swaraj nee Sharma was born on the 14th of February 1952 and died suddenly of a heart attack on the 6th of August 2019 from a heart attack. She was a supreme court lawyer, prior to her entry into the BJP Party under the Narendra Modi government (2014-2019) as the Minister of External affairs of India. She held many prestigious posts at the cabinet and was India's most respected and best loved cabinet minister.

She was of the ilk of Indira Gandhi and her speeches both on the parliament floor and at the UN were delivered in India's official language Sanskrit derived Hindi. She was responsible for implementing the foreign policy of Narendra Modi and was the second female to hold this position after Indira Gandhi. She asked Narendra Modi to declare Ancient India's (Mahabharat) Brahma texts of Bhagavat Gita as India's official book and a must for children to study. As External affairs minister she played a pivotal role and had a strong presence in the ongoing peace negotiations during the civil war in Syria and throughout the Middle east conflicts, as her role in external international affairs she was excellent as an official spokesperson, both on the international stage and domestic. She was latterly given the outstanding Parliamentarian award, and the prestigious Grand cross of Order of civil merit. She left behind her husband a peer and fellow advocate Swaraj Kaushal (supreme courts of India) and her daughter. On 6th August 2019, she suffered a heart attack and later died, of a cardiac arrest. She was given full state honours at the Lodhi crematorium New Delhi, she was of a similar age to Indira Gandhi and had a similar profound influence on international and domestic politics.

Rania of Jordan – Arabia -Middle East

Rania-Al-Yassin-Abdullah the queen consort of Jordan, is Palestinian by her birth and origins. She was educated in Cairo and gained a Batchelors degree there. In 1991, following the Gulf war, her family fled to Jordan, where she met the Prince of Jordan, Prince Abdullah. Before her marriage, she worked in marketing at apple. Her advocacy work as Queen consort, has been related to education, youth empowerment, cross cultural diplomacy, and dialogue. She is on several boards of international bodies, such as Every Child Council, Operation Smile, International Youth Foundation, and as an advocate for suffering children, in the Arabian world and peninsula. She heads various global leadership initiatives and has been recognised as the most beautiful women in the world. Her Husband and King played a powerful role in international diplomacy during the twenty-year conflicts and wars in the Arabian Peninsula, Middle East, and Afghanistan, it is then that she came to prominence on the global stage.

Positive affirmative principle in the United States was intended to end and correct the effects of a specific form of discrimination and actions that resulted from a set of laws, policies, and guidelines. The policy now called affirmative action in the reconstruction era (1863-1877) were raised to restore African workers populations who lacked skills and resources for independent living. It developed through Roosevelt, Truman, Eisenhower, Kennedy, Johnson, Nixon, Ford, Reagan, Obama, and Trump administrations.

There are many arguments against and in favour of the affirmative principle and action, some cites as success for women through the quota systems, to counterbalance inequalities, for native Americans too, but studies have shown that it can create biases in employment and education sectors, elevating minorities whilst still increasing failures. Thus, some of them are like the arguments made by France more against it then for. The quota system some state is not as effective as considered to obliterate inequalities and create a mismatch effect and other anomalies, creating more discrimination, then first intended to remove by the positive affirmative principle.

Human rights are a specific piece of legislation which incorporates the ECHR into French domestic law. The aims of the human rights act are that over time, a shared understanding of what is fundamentally right and wrong, leading people to have more confidence in key state bodies, encourage, better leadership, operating in republics and democracies. France and European states as well as American are no exception. Are the Human rights then an attachment to the values of the constitution and mirrors it? In the UK, by comparison there is no written constitution, certain precedents conventions and customs take its place. A few principles are in a form that are then integral to the unwritten constitution, such as parliamentary sovereignty, the rule of law and separation of powers. The absence of an all-encompassing written law, to which all other laws, administrative, decisions and common law, must and should be the mandate of the legal order be interpreted to conform, marks the decisions, in French,

European, and in the Anglo-American systems. The HR is an added guidance about natural justice norms of right and wrong, and which now courts are guided by to interpret statutes, administrative decisions, and the common law to be aligned with natural justice, the original leading light or charter, through which human fundamental notions of right versus wrong should direct domestic, national, and international laws. The highest standard based on natural justice norms are the basic features of life of right and wrong codified within the three or four pillars of the legal order which are first and foremost the constitutional principles and through which laws statutes, rights are made and directed, never overstepping the boundaries of classic principles, nor interfering with them in negative ways that may impact the boundaries, remedies and restrict the natural sovereignty of human beings as natural persons, first and foremost. The constitutional principles are embodied in all things therefore, the constitutional laws, constitutional like effects. Human right credibility, credentials.

The French constitutional principles mandates that while determining legal questions, including developments, the three branches of government, including courts, must consider.

The constitutional principles have enshrined within them higher laws, and they universally mandate, that while determining legal questions, as in France, like paritary, or other modern, legal developments, the constitution must consider the higher law, constitutional principles, the scope of which is embodied in laws, statutes, human rights, civil liberties, as these stem from them. The constitution mandates in France and challenging in the USA that statutes, legal instruments, of all kinds, must be read and given effect in a way that is compatible with higher principles. Its provisions relating to declarations of incompatibility. The courts may consider through arguments, relating to compatibility of both primary and secondary legislation.

If the primary legal instruments legislation cannot or is not correctly placed in the legal order, and if the laws made cannot be interpreted to be compatible with higher principles, the courts are obliged to declare such as incompatible. If a secondary legal instrument suffers from a similar fault, the directing or governing constitutional or the primary legislation prevents the fault from being duly remedied, short of revocation. The court may declare such legislation too incompatible turnover if the secondary legislation incompatible.

Moreover, if the secondary or derived legislation or primary is not compatible the courts have the power to strike it out, provided no other legal instrument prevents this. Thus, a declaration of incompatibility can affect latter validity, enforcement, or continuing operation of the legislation, and the law may remain, till the incompatibility is removed. And thus, the authorities move to amend the law.

The constitutional principles are at the apex of the legal order and the fundamental thesis for the formation of all legal instruments, and directives on permitted human rights of note. Its mandates that supreme courts, courts of appeal must be given the power to make declarations of incompatibility. Lower courts who they hear matters where in cases, principles or higher justice laws have been breached, adjust, although they may not have the power to pass declarations of incompatibility.

Once a declaration of incompatibility is triggered, it enables officials of government to make remedial orders to amend legislation and bring instruments and rights to align with principles.

The question of legislative incompatibility is raised in proceedings in parliaments, and congress, and senate floors, and this enables the government to clarify its stance.

The constitutional thesis and principles mandate from their original construction, that an official authority will not have acted unlawfully if as a result of a declaration one or more provisions of primary legislation the office could not have acted differently. A granting of remedy must be just and appropriate while ministers can amend the relevant legislation. There are mandates for protection of rights to expression, privacy, and any derogations and reservations must be listed at the time or making or entering treaties, reservations can be made, which occur, frequently and these can subsist for a term or lower and can be reviewed before they are applied. These must be laid before the senate, or parliament, all courts must make note of changes. Core public bodies which are manifestly central govt departments, local authorities, those in possession of general or special powers, who are registered for democratic accountability, and there is an obligation to act in the interests of human rights but equally in the public interests. Constitutional principles must be given judicial deference, through appreciation, and critical imperatives. Courts must at all times, and legislators must balance this due deference, with intentions, which enacting a statute and the rights of individuals and political rights. Not all issues, are equal, some involve matters, of social and public policy, whilst all involve higher laws, or constitutional principles. All convention rights are not equal, some absolute, some qualified other limited.

The major universal rights within legal orders are the basic fundamental rights, right to life, not be tortured, freedom from forced labour, right to liberty, fair trials, no punishment without law, respect for private family life, home and correspondence, freedom of thought, conscience, religion, expression, freedom of belief, assembly association, marriage and forming a family, anti-discrimination, with respect to human dignity, right to education, free elections, enjoyment of possessions, and parity rights, for higher office for women. There are still protocols to sign and ratify, civil imprisonment, free movement, restriction of death penalty, crime and family procedural and institutional protocols.

These are acknowledged to have a considerable impact on public law, and judicial review can be made of executive actions, including policies, decisions, legislations, order, or decisions.

The principal grounds are made not on a reconsideration of facts but a fresh decision on merits, appeals substitutes, for original decisions. These can be illegality, errors in law, purpose used for granting law, powers ignorant of relevant considerations or taking irrelevant considerations into account or fettering discretion equally irrationality, proportionality, or procedural impropriety, in statutory procedures, breach of natural justice, rules against bias, and the duty required to give reasons.

Through all of this, then the USA for the first time, has a female Vice President. How will this change the future of politics and the lot of minority actors in politics and does this then pave the way for a female President of the USA, some say its time has come. So, who is Kamala Harris, and what does she stand for, to have earned such a unique spot in American Politics and will she make a huge impact and difference? So far, we know who she is, but her achievements will only be recorded, by the passing of time, at the end of her term of High Office.

Vice President Kamala Harris - North America – United States of America – USA

Kamala Harris, was born 1964, is the first female vice President, and the highest ranking female official in US History, she is of Indian and Jamaican origins. Her mother and father were both academics and she is a trained attorney in law. She rose to instant fame, with President Joseph Biden the 46th President of the USA, by declaring the end of a twenty-year conflict in Afghanistan, which was started post 9/11 in the hunt for Osama Bin Laden, the perpetrator of the crimes against America.

References

Article 89 of the constitution of the Vth French Republic.

Blacker Phillippe Droit constitutional de identite feminine Revue administrative, 1996, p38.

Convention on the elimination of all forms of discrimination against women of 17th December 1979.

Council Directive 76/207/EEC 9 Feb 1976.

European convention on the protection of human rights and fundamental liberties of 4th November 1950.

High Drama as Women's Bill is introduced in the Lok Sabha – The Times of India, December 12th, 1999.

Hague, Rod, Martin Harrop, Shawn Breslin – Comparative government and politics, an introduction, fourth edition, Macmillan, Press Ltd, 1998, p131.

Hine David – Political Parties; development of in the Blackwell encyclopaedia of Political science p 411.

Jorge Marinda – Manual de Direi to Constitutional, vol iv Lisboa, 1988 p 219.

Jeffrey Olin, Vincent Barry, applying Ethics, sixth edition, Wadworth Publishing company, Belmont USA 1990 p 373.

Lafolette Hugh, Ethics in practice, An Anthology, Blackwell Publishers, Cambridge (USA) Oxford 1997, p 429.

Madhu Kishmar, 'Women's marginal role in politics in enhancing women's representation in legislatures. An alternative to the government Bill for Women's representation form for democratic reforms.

Report of the Committee on status of women in India 1976 pp 302 – 305.

Universal suffrage just adopted second republic (1848-1851).

French Constitution

The constitution of 1791 adopted 3 September 1791, established the Kingdom of the French, a constitutional Monarchy, and the legislative Assembly.

The charter of 1830 established the July Monarchy.

French Constitution, of 1848, established the French Republic.

The French constitution of 1958 established the French Republic.

The French Constitution of 1958 established the French, Fifth Republic.

Affirmative Principle and actions USA landmark Cases and articles.

Anderson Elizabeth S – Rawls John, Thurnall Arthur F July 2008, Race, Gender, and Affirmative Action, University of Michigan, June 4, 2020.

Grigg V Duke Power company 401 US 424 (1971).

Grutter V Bollinger 539 US 306 (2003).

Morton V Mancani 417 US 535 (1974).

Student for fair admissions V University of Texas at Austin (2021).

United States v Fordice 505 US 717.

Wygant V Jackson Board of Education (1986).

EU Law

A O'Neill, EU Law for UK Lawyers (Hart 2011)

C Barnard, The substantive Law of the EU, the four freedoms fourth edition 2013

G Beck, the legal reasoning of the court of Justice of the EU (Hart 2013).

P Craig and D de Burca – EU Law: Text cases and materials (6th Edition 2015).

C Tobbler and J Begleyer, Essential EU Law in charts fourth edition 2018

J H H Weiler, the transformation of Europe (1991) (8) Yale Law Journal 2403 EU architecture only found in the Federal States.

T Hartley, The foundations of European Union (2014).

- The Life of Indira Nehru Gandhi by Katherine Frank
- Speeches and writings by Indira Gandhi
- Daughter of Destiny by Benazir Bhutto.
- The changing Portrayal of Asma Al Assad in the western media by Inga Van Derstein.
- Angela Merkel by Stefan Kornelius.
- Freedom from fear by Aung San Suu Kyi

Human Right Act

Structure of the European convention on Human Rights and Protocols

European convention on Human Rights convention for the protection of Human rights and fundamental freedoms

Protocol No 6 to the convention for the protection of Human rights and fundamental freedoms concerning the abolition of the death penalty

Protocol seven to the convention for the protection of human rights and fundamental freedoms.

Protocol No 12 to the convention for the protection of Human Rights and fundamental freedoms.

Protocol No 13 to the convention for the protection of Human Rights and fundamental freedoms concerning the abolition of the death penalty in all circumstances.

Http://conventions.coe.int/Treaty/Html/005.htm.

http://w.w.w.echr.coe.int/nr/r/d5cc24a7-dc13-4318-b457-5c9014916d7a/0englishanglais.pdf

http://conventions.coe.int/treaty/commun/ListeTraites.asp?MA=44&CM+7&CL=ENG

About the Author

Dr Amrit Rattan K Baidwan-Macfarland – studied public law, French constitution and governance, international relations, as part of her legal studies. She is a qualified scientist-Jurist-Lawyer, with an interest in public law and foreign affairs and trained in criminal litigation, Human rights with her law firms in Scotland, and did a short secondment to India shadowing members of the Attorney General's department and gaining insights into commonwealth legal systems. She also undertook, the study of American legal subjects involving comparative analysis, between two jurisdictions, Scots and American. She gained deep insights in theoretical and pragmatic foreign policy, relations, and affairs, from her academic engagements with the universities in Scotland, as well as universities in Washington, USA. She enjoyed her research in conflict studies, peace, and security as part of the contemporary living history modules. Through these subjects, the evolving character of global and supranational institutions could be gleaned, as well as the interpretation of civic societies and international diplomacy, exploration of juristic constitutionalism at national and international levels, peace, conflict, and the role of religious principles in the Arabian Peninsula.

Selected Publications

MacFarland A.K., 2019 – Against the death penalty, the philosophies of *Supreme Court Justice Stephen Breyer*, Justinian, Kant, Gandhi, Confucius, Roman legal scholars and Jurists – Book Chapter in ISBN 978-1-7283-8330-9.

MacFarland A.K., 2019 - Signal transduction at the blood brain barrier, book chapter ISBN 978-1-7283-8629-4.

MacFarland, A.K., Dawson, A & Pearson, C.K. Analysis of MDR1 and MDR3 gene expression and amplification in consecutive samples in patients with Acute Leukaemia. Leukemia Lymphoma, 19 (1-2): 135-140.

MacFarland, A.K., Ewen, S.B. & Pearson, C.K. Stage Specific distribution of P-glycoprotein in first term and full term human placenta. Histochemical Journal 26:417 -423.

Lewis, R.J., **MacFarland, A.K.,** Anandavijayan, S., Aspden R.M. Site variation of material properties and metabolic activity of articular cartilage from the bovine carpometacarpal joint. Osteoarthritis and Cartilage 6, 383 -392.

MacFarland, A.K., The role of molecular biology in Orthopaedic surgery. Current Orthopaedics. 11, 281 -287.

MacFarland, A.K., Gene Therapy principles in Orthopaedics, Current Orthopaedics July 2000 Vol 14 Issue 4 pages 278-283.

McFarland, A.K., Ewen, S.B., & Pearson C.K., Development and Analysis of a novel leukaemic cell line resistant to Daunorubicin and Vincristine Sulphate in combination abstract and conference proceedings Banff Canada.

McFarland, A.K., Gordon, M.J., & Dutta-Roy, A.K., Mechanical Load stimulates prostaglandin E2 synthesis by articular cartilage chondrocytes in vitro paper in Conference proceedings, Israel Jerusalem.

MacFarland A.K., Hoyland, J.A., Ewen, S.B. Localization and characterization of the response of chondrocytes to mechanical load using the in situ hybridization –conference proceedings and abstract, Israel Jerusaleum.

MacFarland, A.K., Bovine knee joint meniscus. Metabolic response to compressive loads in vitro. Conference proceedings and abstract in Lyon France.

MacFarland, A.K., Gordon, M.J., Dutta-Roy, A.K. Mechanical Load stimulates prostaglandin in E2 synthesis by articular cartilage chondrocytes in vitro. Matrix Biol. 15: 172.

MacFarland, A.K., Lewis, R.R.J., Regulation of articular cartilage extracellular matrix biosynthesis. Cytokine 7:660.

MacFarland, A.K., Ewen - The effect of mechanical load on cytokine gene expression in bovine and articular cartilage analyzed by messenger RNA phenotyping. International Journal of Experimental Pathology 76: A26.

MacFarland A.K., Ewan A., Aignar, T., Keenan, G., Cordiner, D - Localization and Characterisation of the response of chondrocytes to mechanical load using in situ Hybridization. Matrix 114:378.

MacFarland A.K., and Ewen S.W. The TGFBeta Signalling Pathway: Augmenting Meniscal repair? Second Smith and Nephew International Symposium, Conference proceedings and published abstract – Tissue Engineering 2000 – Advances in Tissue Engineering 2000 – Advances in Tissue Engineering Biomaterials and Cell Signalling. University of York.

MacFarland, A.K., Dutta-Roy, A.K Induction of 1L-1Beta and PGE-2 in articular cartilage by static compressive loads. Conference proceedings and published abstract in Biomechanics of Articular Cartilage and related Topics on its Structure and Biochemistry: Leeds, UK.

MacFarland, A.K., Dutta-Roy, A.K, Endogenous production of prostaglandin E2 in human articular cartilage stimulate by physiological compressive loads in situ Conference proceedings and published abstract in Connective Tissue Society, Oxford, UK.

MacFarland, A.K., Gordon, M.J., Dutta-Roy, A.K, Physiological compressive loads stimulate prostaglandin E2 synthesis by human articular cartilage in vitro. Conference proceedings and published abstract in British Connective Tissue Society, Oxford, UK.

MacFarland, A.K., Dutta-Roy, A.K., Production of prostaglandin E2 by human articular cartilage explants in response to physiological compressive loads: a potential regulator of endogenous IL-1Beta formation. Conference proceedings and peer reviewed published abstract in 7th SICOT Trainees Meeting, Charing Cross, London, 28-30 November.

MacFarland, A.K., Expression *of PDGFBeta and TGFbeta* in cyclic and static loaded human cartilage explants. Conference proceedings and peer reviewed published abstract in Bone and Cartilage repair. 5th Annual Meeting of the European Tissue Repair Society, Padova, Italy, September.

MacFarland A.K., - response of articular chondrocytes to mechanical load. Conference proceedings and published abstract in the Royal National Orthopaedic journal, - Hospital, Stanmore, University.

MacFarland, A.K., Regulation of chondrocyte metabolism by mechanical loading ex vivo and in vitro –Conference proceedings and published abstract in XIV FECTS Meeting, Lyon, France, September.

MacFarland, A.K., Multidrug resistance mechanisms in a novel leukaemia cell line. Conference proceedings and published abstract in British Drug Resistance Meeting, Manchester, UK.

MacFarland, A.K., Isolation and identification of the cytokine – eicosanoid pathway in chondrocytes. Published abstract – presentation at *Cleveland Ohio, USA.*

MacFarland, A.K., Cytokine gene expression in articular cartilage in response to mechanical load. Published abstract and peer reviewed presentation at *Roslin Institute, Midlothian and University of Edinburgh.*

MacFarland, A.K., Development of novel cell line resistant to combination chemotherapy using Daunorubicin and Vincristine Sulphate – published abstract and peer reviewed presentation at *Sloane Kettering Cancer Institute, New York, USA.*

MacFarland, A.K., Development of novel cell line resistant to combination chemotherapy using Daunorubicin and Vincristine Sulphate. Published abstract and peer reviewed presentation at Birmingham *University (Queen Elizabeth Hospital CRC unite.*

MacFarland, A.K., Development of novel cell line resistant to combination chemotherapy using Daunorubicin and Vincristine Sulphate. *PhD departmental presentation and peer review - Aberdeen University (molecular and Cell Biology), UK.*

MacFarland, A.K., *Regulatory effects of exogenous cytokines IL-1Beta and TNF-alpha on the synthesis of neutral metalloproteases in Human Articular Cartilage Explants. Conference proceedings and abstract, Second Smith and Nephew International Symposium Tissue Engineering, Advances in Tissue Engineering Biomaterials and Cell Signalling.* **York, UK.**

MacFarland A.K., *Signal mechanotransduction from membrane receptors to the chondrocytes nucleus (IL-1 beta-PGE2) a cytokine – eicosanoid pathway. Third International Colloquim on "Cellular Signal Recognition and Transduction", Conference proceedings and abstract,* **Berlin Germany.**

MacFarland, A.K., *Endogenous production of prostaglandin E2 in human articular cartilage stimulated by physiological compressive loads in vitro. Conference proceeding and abstract - 14*[th] *Annual Orthopaedic Residents Conference,* **Memphis, USA.**

MacFarland, A.K., *Mechanical load stimulated prostaglandin E2 synthesis by articular cartilage chondrocytes in vitro. Conference proceedings and published abstract VI International Conference on the Molecular Biology and Pathology of Matrix, Philadelphia.*

MacFarland, A.K., *Inducible expression of multidrug resistance genes in CCRF-HSB2 leukaemic cells in response to the cytotoxic drugs Daunorubicin and Vincristine investigated using differential display RT-PCR. Inducible Genome Response,* **Conference proceedings and published abstract Oregon, USA.**

MacFarland, A.K., Lewis R. *Human articular explant culture under loading conditions – an appropriate in vitro model to study synthesis and regulation of normal human cartilage. Conference proceedings and published abstract at 5th Annual Meeting or European Tissue repair Society – **Padova, Italy.***

MacFarland, A.K., *Regulation of chondrocytes metabolism by mechanical loading ex vivo and in vitro. XVI FECTS Conference proceedings and published abstract – **Lyon, France.***

MacFarland, A.K., Ewen, S., Hoyland, J. A., Aigner, T., Keenan, G., Cordiner D, *Localization and characterization of the response of chondrocytes to mechanical load using in situ hybridization. Conference proceedings and published abstract Vth International Conference on the molecular Biology and Pathology of Matrix. II-25. **Philadelphia, USA.***

MacFarland, A.K., Mellor, S., Abranovich, D.R., Ewen, S.B., Tsuruo, T., & Pearson, C.K. *Expression of P-glycoprotein in human placenta and foetal tissues. Conference proceedings and published abstract at AACR Special Conference in Cancer Research (membrane transport in multidrug resistance development and disease) B-11., **Banff, Canada.***

About the Book

The promulgation of the French constitution and its key and fundamental concept of Universalism marked the end of Monarchical rule in France, and the fifth republican constitution, similarly marked the end of its fundamental and evolutionary history. The French constitution influenced the American line American, Australian, European nations states, governance philosophy and constitutions. These were founded on its stability, and the dynamics of governance, became a settled matter as amendments rested in and through its final stages. There was a resurgence of classical elements, principles, within the legal order of nations, and social, economic, and environmental contexts were impacted. This book focuses on the rights to high office, by women, through the lens of the foundations of the French universalism concept, but also does a comparative analysis of the American affirmative principle, differentialism, European human rights and charters, using notable examples from throughout the world, the Atlantic, Pacific and African-Arabian spheres, such as Indira Gandhi, Angela Merkel, Aung San Suu Kyi and the recently appointed Vice President of USA Kamala Harris.